NATIVE HOMES

Bobbie Kalman

🌱 Crabtree Publishing Company

www.crabtreebooks.com

NATIVE HOMES

Created by Bobbie Kalman

(Dedicated by Bonna Rouse)
To my parents for their loving support

Author and Editor-in-Chief
Bobbie Kalman

Research and editing
Deanna Brady
Niki Walker

Copy editors
Heather Fitzpatrick
Kathryn Smithyman

Computer and Graphic design
Kymberley McKee Murphy

Production coordinator
Heather Fitzpatrick

Consultants
Jackie Labonte, Literacy Coordinator,
    Niagara Regional Native Centre
Deanna Brady, Corporate Board Director, PHO 2000
    American Indian Outreach Programs; American
    Indian Changing Spirits
Professor J.S. Milloy, The Frost Centre for Canadian
    and Native Studies, Trent University

Photographs and reproductions
The Greenwich Workshop, Inc. Shelton, CT:
    Tom Lovell, *Pecos Pueblo, About 1500* (detail),
    pages 6-7; *The Gift* (detail), 18;
    The Helpers (detail), 22, back cover
Bobbie Kalman, page 15
© Permission of Lazare & Parker: pages 12, 13, 14,
    24 (top), 28, 31 (right)
Alfredo Rodriguez, page 25 (bottom)
© Craig Tennant, page 21 (top)

Illustrations
Barbara Bedell: cover, pages 18 (bottom), 19 (top),
    22 (top), 24 (bottom), 29
Bonna Rouse: interior backgrounds, pages 4-5, 8-9,
    10-11, 15, 16 (bottom), 20, 23, 25 (top), 26
Margaret Amy Reiach: pages 4-5 (underground log
    lodge, bark wigwams & chickee), 9 (insets),
    10-11 (border), 16 (top), 17, 19 (bottom & center),
    21 (bottom), 26 (pots), 30, 31 (left), back cover hide

Crabtree Publishing Company

www.crabtreebooks.com   1-800-387-7650

PMB16A	612 Welland Ave.	73 Lime Walk
350 Fifth Ave.	St. Catharines	Headington
Suite 3308	Ontario	Oxford
New York, NY	Canada	OX3 7AD
10118	L2M 5V6	United Kingdom

Cataloging in Publication Data
Kalman, Bobbie
    Native homes / Bobbie Kalman
        p. cm. -- (Native nations of North America)
    Includes index.
    ISBN 0-7787-0371-1 (RLB) -- ISBN 0-7787-0463-7 (pbk.)
    This book introduces children to the traditional dwellings built
and used by Native nations across North America.
    1. Indians of North America--Dwellings--Juvenile literature.
[1. Indians of North America--Dwellings.] I. Title. II. Series.
E98.D9 K35 2001
392.3'608997--dc21
                                                            LC00-069362
                                                            CIP

CONTENTS

Native homes

Thousands of years before the United States or Canada were countries, hundreds of groups of people lived throughout North America. These peoples were North America's first, or **indigenous**, peoples. They are known as Native peoples, First Nations, original peoples, aboriginal peoples, Indians, and Native Americans, but they prefer to be called by the names of their **nations**, or groups. Each of the hundreds of Native nations in North America has its own language and culture.

Yesterday and today

Today, most Native people live in the same types of homes as those of other people. In the past, however, they built traditional homes, or **lodges**, that suited their surroundings and lifestyles and the climate of the areas in which they lived. Wherever they lived, Native people always built their homes from natural materials.

A variety of lodges

In cool, wooded areas such as the Northeast and Northwest, people built large permanent homes using tree trunks. In the Great Plains and Southwest, there was not much wood, so people made homes using grasses, mud, and stone. Some built basic wooden frames and covered them with animal hides. In warm, wet areas such as the Southeast, homes were often made without walls. The roofs were constructed of woven plants, which kept the dwellings dry while allowing air to circulate. Even in the Far North, where few plants grow, Native people found ways to make homes using whale bones, caribou hides, and blocks of snow.

*Each Native nation had its own language and lived in a specific **homeland**. This map of North America's major geographic regions shows some of the traditional lodges built by Native peoples.*

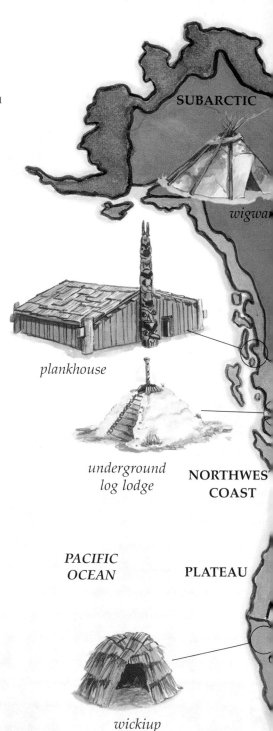

SUBARCTIC

wigwam

plankhouse

underground log lodge

NORTHWEST COAST

PACIFIC OCEAN

PLATEAU

wickiup

thatched home

4

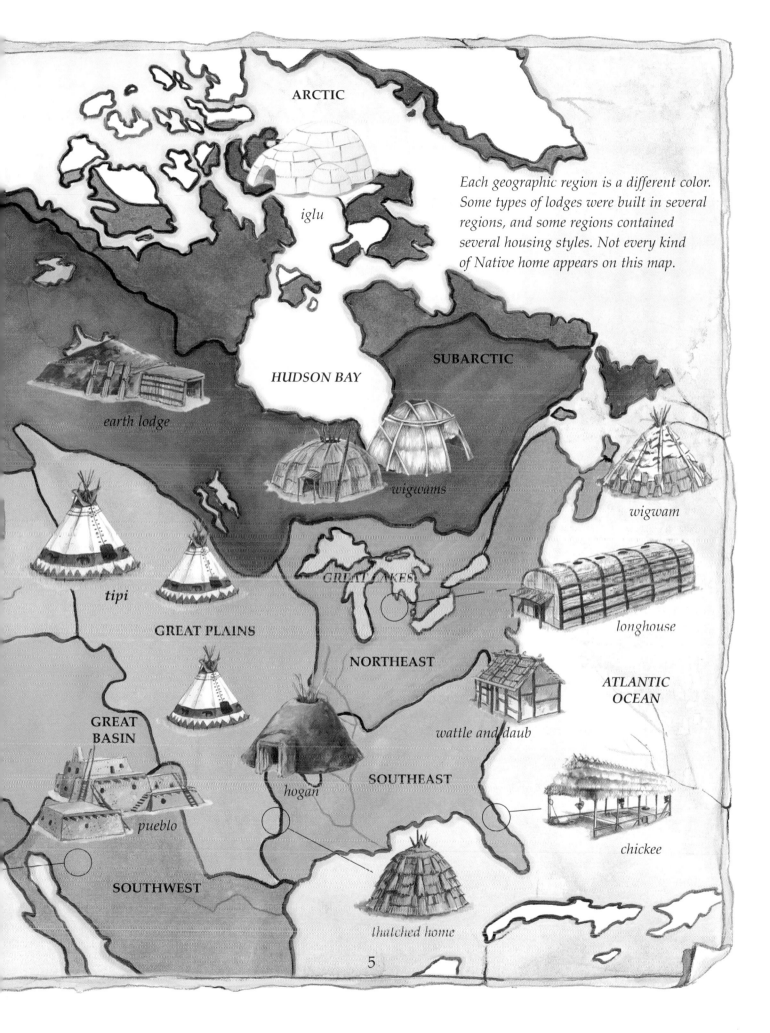

ARCTIC

iglu

Each geographic region is a different color. Some types of lodges were built in several regions, and some regions contained several housing styles. Not every kind of Native home appears on this map.

HUDSON BAY

SUBARCTIC

earth lodge

wigwams

wigwam

tipi

GREAT LAKES

longhouse

GREAT PLAINS

NORTHEAST

ATLANTIC OCEAN

GREAT BASIN

wattle and daub

pueblo

hogan

SOUTHEAST

chickee

SOUTHWEST

thatched home

Different lifestyles

Lifestyle was an important factor in the type of housing people built. In areas with poor soil or little water, Native **bands**, or groups, relied on hunting for survival. These **nomadic** people, who moved from place to place, followed animal herds and lived in temporary camps. Their shelters resembled tents.

Easy-to-carry homes

Many of the nations that lived on the Great Plains relied on buffalo for food and used their hides to make clothing and shelter. When the buffalo moved during different seasons, the people followed them. Their homes, called **tipis**, were easy to assemble and light enough to be moved to new locations.

Sedentary nations

People who lived in areas with rich soil and a good water supply were usually **sedentary**—they stayed in one place. Most grew crops such as corn, beans, and pumpkins, but they also made short hunting and fishing trips. They built permanent homes, such as the **pueblo** shown on the opposite page.

© Tom Lovell

A longhouse village

In the northeastern woodlands, most of the Iroquoian-speaking nations, such as the Haudenosaunee, Wendat, Erie, and Neutral, were sedentary. They lived in permanent homes called **longhouses**. A longhouse is a large rectangular building with a framework of wooden poles covered with bark. Villages were made up of several longhouses surrounded by a wooden wall. They were built in clearings in the woods and on the banks of rivers and streams. Many were located high on hilltops for extra protection.

*Villages were enclosed by protective walls called **palisades**. Longhouses caught fire easily, so they were built in a random pattern to prevent fires from spreading.*

The home of a clan

A longhouse was the home of a **clan**, or extended family, whose members were related to a common female ancestor. Clans often carved their **emblem**, or symbol, over the front door to identify their home. The emblem was an animal such as a turtle or wolf. A clan was named after an animal that was important to the clan or lived in its homeland.

Building a longhouse

The men shared the work of constructing the longhouse. Before they began construction, they went into the woods to peel bark off young trees and find long, thin tree trunks. They laid the bark flat to dry and cut it into large sheets. They used the trunks to make poles. On a flat area of ground, they traced the outline of the house, dug holes along it, and set the poles into the holes. The poles were the framework for the outer walls.

The frame and roof

To make the frame stronger, the men also lashed poles across the inside. For the roof, they fastened poles to the top of the walls, slanted them toward the center, and tied them together. The roof was sloped so that snow would slide off. The frame was covered with sheets of bark turned rough-side out and tied with bark strips. The overlapping sheets of bark kept out the wind and rain.

Longhouses had a doorway at one or both ends of the building, which was covered by a flap of bark. Some doorways were shaded by bark awnings.

Inside a longhouse

The longhouse was divided in half by a wide corridor that stretched from one end to the other. On either side of the corridor were sections, which were used by individual families. Each section was about thirteen feet (4 meters) long. The sections were separated by work areas. Several fireplaces were dug into the ground along the corridor. Families who lived across from one another shared a fireplace.

Separate compartments

Families often hung woven screens at the sides of their sections for privacy. They also hung mats or hides at the front, but in winter, most left the compartments open to enjoy the heat from the fireplaces.

A place to sit or sleep

Each compartment had two or three wide platforms attached to the wall. People used the platforms for sitting, working, and storing items such as food, tools, clothing, and firewood. They also slept on these platforms, using cornhusk mattresses. In winter, they covered themselves with bearskin blankets.

Storage room

Families stored food and personal possessions on their shelves or under their platforms. Many longhouses also had storage pits dug into the earthen floors. These were lined with bark and filled with corn, meat, and other foods. Some foods were hung from the rafters or storage racks to keep them away from mice and other pests.

No need to lock doors

Longhouse dwellers did not worry about leaving their possessions unattended in the longhouse because people rarely stole.

Tools, weapons, snowshoes, and fur blankets were hung along the longhouse walls and inside the compartments. Baskets lined the top shelves.

Smoky interiors

Winters could be harsh in the northeastern woodlands, so villagers spent a lot of time indoors huddled around the warm fireplaces.

When it rained or snowed, the smoke holes in the roof were closed and the longhouse filled with smoke. The smoke stung people's eyes and made it difficult to breathe comfortably.

11

Woodland wigwam camps

Before the Europeans came, Algonkian-speaking people lived all over North America, from the Atlantic to the Rocky Mountains, as far north as the Arctic, and as far south as Tennessee. Algonkian nations were hunters and fishers who did little farming. They set up seasonal camps, following herds of animals.

Temporary homes

In the wooded areas around the Great Lakes and East Coast, some Algonkian nations lived in longhouses like those of the Iroquoians, but most, such as the Anishinabe (Ojibwe), lived in **wigwams**. A wigwam has a rounded, rectangular, or cone frame made of thin, curved, wooden poles with large sheets of tree bark or animal hides sewn over it.

Building a wigwam

To build a wigwam, the builder's first job was to trace an outline on the ground and then dig holes along it. The poles that made up the frame would be set into these holes, making the wigwam sturdier. The poles were the stripped trunks of flexible young trees. Each pole had a partner directly across from it, and the pairs were curved to meet at the top in an arch. Each pair was tied together with basswood strips. The builder reinforced it with two or three rows of poles. Once the frame was secure, the cover was put on.

(above) While some people at this camp are busy building a wigwam, others are preparing meat from the hunt by cooking some of it and smoking the rest over a fire.

Layers of coverings

With the frames already in place, people had only to attach the coverings, and their wigwams were ready. The covering of the wigwam was made up of a few layers, especially in winter. The inner layer consisted of sheets of birch or elm bark, animal hides, or woven leaves, which the women stitched together with strips of basswood. The roof was made of overlapping sheets of bark, which were lightweight and water resistant. An opening in the roof allowed smoke from the campfire to escape. The hole was covered by a flap of bark that could be opened and closed with a long pole.

Easy to move

When people left one campsite for another, they removed the covering of their wigwam and left the frame in place for when they would return. They carried the bark or hides with them from campsite to campsite. These materials were lightweight and could be carried easily from one location to another.

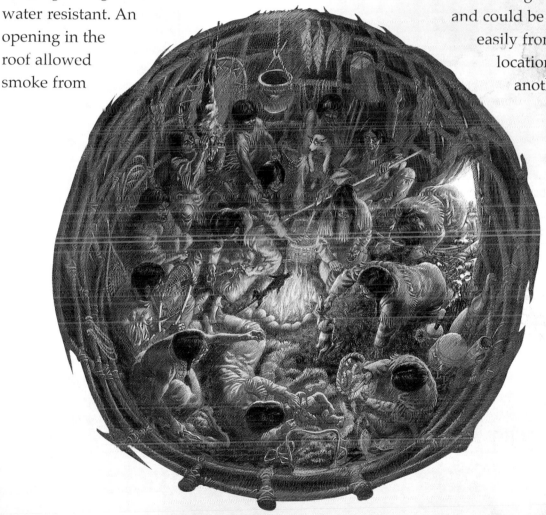

This bird's-eye view shows the interior of a wigwam, which is shared by more than one family. The floor is covered with pine needles. For safety, the fire is surrounded by stones and there is a smoke hole above it. People crawl in and out through a low doorway. Several activities take place inside—making snowshoes, stripping a fox pelt, shafting a spear, and cooking food. Life in this wigwam is busy and cosy!

13

Other Algonkian homes

Algonkian-speaking peoples built many kinds of wigwams. The Penobscots, who lived in the coastal areas of what is now Maine, and the Mi'kmaqs (Micmacs), who inhabited Nova Scotia, Prince Edward Island, and New Brunswick, built conical, square, or rounded dwellings of bark and hides. These east-coast nomadic people hunted caribou, otter, moose, and beaver, as well as seals and walruses. They fished and collected shellfish along the seashore. They used the furs and hides of animals to make clothing and bedding and the bones to make tools and weapons.

This illustration shows a hunting and fishing camp being set up on the shore of a waterway. Some people are building shelters, and others are drawing their clan emblems on the bark of their lodge before the final poles are added to secure the frame. One woman is tanning a hide, and others are cooking supper. The people on the right of the picture are collecting branches for building wigwams and for making a fire. Many of the men at the camp are fishing, and some are building a bark canoe. Name other activities that you see taking place at this busy camp.

"Air-conditioned" homes

The North Carolina Algonkians, such as the Moratok, Secotan, and Chowanoc, lived in areas with a mild climate. They built villages that resembled the longhouse villages of the Iroquoians, but the building materials they used were different.

Winters were not as cold as those of the northern woodlands, and the summers were quite hot. Instead of bark, the curved-roof "longhouse" wigwams of these Algonkians were covered with woven mats that could be pulled down in cold weather and rolled up in warm weather to allow breezes to blow through. The Powhatan nation of Virginia lived in similar wigwams, as shown in the inset photograph.

Abundant land

The area in which these people lived had bountiful forests, rivers teeming with fish, and rich soil that could be farmed easily. People hunted and fished, but they also grew crops such as corn, beans, melons, sunflowers, pumpkins, and tobacco, which was used for special ceremonies.

These long wigwam homes were comfortable, and the wood and grasses used to build them were easy to find. On hunting trips, these people used smaller wigwams.

Thatched homes

In warm areas of North America, many Native nations built **thatched** homes or homes with thatched roofs. Thatch is a covering made up of layers of leaves, grasses, reeds, or straw. Thatch helps keep out rain and wind, but it allows air to circulate inside the dwelling. Thatched homes include the **wickiup**, **chickee**, **wattle and daub**, and **lean-to**. These dwellings were most commonly used in the Southeast and the area that is now California.

The wikiup

A wickiup has a wooden dome-shaped frame. It is sometimes known as a brush hut, grass hut, or tule hut, depending on the plants that are used to cover it. In warm areas such as California, wickiups were often used year-round. In cooler areas, they were used as temporary shelters. When the thatch wore out, the wickiup was burned and a new one was built.

The Chumash of Southern California were not farmers—they were hunters and gatherers of roots, seeds, berries, and acorns. They lived in wickiups. The frames of the huts were covered in overlapping layers of thatch to keep out rain. The Chumash used cone-shaped reed boats for fishing and travel.

The chickee

Chickees were traditionally used by nations who lived in tropical regions, including the Seminole nation of Florida. A chickee consisted of a square or rectangular frame topped with a peaked roof. The frame was made of cypress logs, and the roof was thatched with woven palmetto leaves or other plants. The side walls were left open to allow breezes to circulate freely.

Chickees can be put up and taken down quickly— a useful feature for bands that relocated frequently.

Wattle and daub

In cooler areas, some nations built houses similar to chickees, but these homes had walls. To make the walls, people often wove a base of twigs and plastered it with mud or clay. This construction is known as **wattle and daub**. The wattle is the woven part, and the daub is the mud plaster.

The lean-to

A lean-to, shown below right, was used by many nations across the continent as temporary housing during short hunting, fishing, or gathering trips. A lean-to was one of the easiest shelters to build. It consists of a simple two-sided frame that resembles an upside-down "V." The frame was made of wooden poles that were covered in thatch. In some areas, these shelters were covered with bark, mats of woven leaves, or hides instead of thatch.

Wattle-and-daub homes were warmer and sturdier than the chickees that had no walls.

This lean-to has been drawn to show its wooden frame and three types of coverings— bark, thatch, and hides.

© Tom Lovell

Portable tipi homes

Many nomadic nations on the Great Plains, such as the Lakota Sioux and Cheyenne, lived in large portable **tipis**. A tipi belonged to the woman of the family, and it was her job to set it up and take it down at each campsite. When not assembled, tipis were compact and lightweight, making it easy to move them from place to place.

Before European settlers brought horses to North America, Plains people used small tipis that could be dragged by their dogs. When the Plains nations acquired horses, they could transport larger tipis. The ability to move bigger shelters and more belongings allowed people to travel farther and set up large village-like camps.

Different coverings

Cone-shaped tents were used as temporary shelters in many areas. Whereas people of the Plains covered their tipis with buffalo hides, other peoples used materials found in their regions, such as grass, bark, or fur.

Decorated tipis

Some tipis were covered with art. The paints were made from items found in nature such as charcoal, plants, animal dung, and powdered rocks. These special tipis often belonged to chiefs or **medicine men**. Sometimes the paintings depicted events but, most often, they represented dreams or visions that the men had seen while praying.

Building a Plains tipi

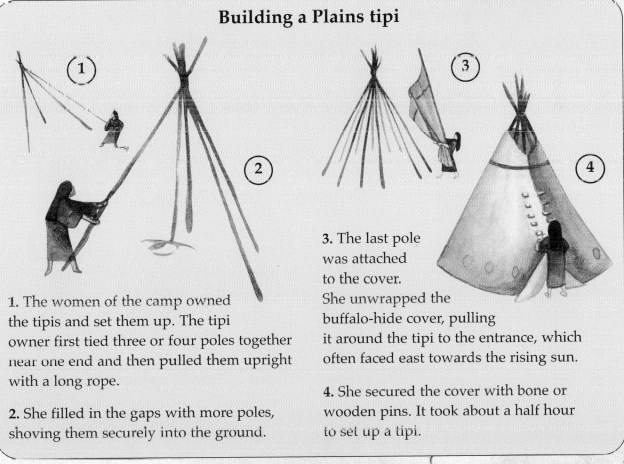

1. The women of the camp owned the tipis and set them up. The tipi owner first tied three or four poles together near one end and then pulled them upright with a long rope.

2. She filled in the gaps with more poles, shoving them securely into the ground.

3. The last pole was attached to the cover. She unwrapped the buffalo-hide cover, pulling it around the tipi to the entrance, which often faced east towards the rising sun.

4. She secured the cover with bone or wooden pins. It took about a half hour to set up a tipi.

Inside a tipi

On the open plains and prairies, temperatures often dropped to freezing, and strong winds whipped across the flat land during winter. Summer temperatures soared as the scorching sun beat down. Despite the extreme weather, however, families stayed comfortable inside their tipis. In summer, women left a wide gap between the ground and the cover, which allowed fresh breezes to blow through the tipi. In winter, they added another layer of hide to the cover and stuffed moss or grass between the layers for extra insulation. They pulled the lining snug against the ground to block the wind.

Everything in its place

Everyone and everything had a certain spot within the tipi. Beds were arranged around the fire, and clothing and tools were placed among them. The position of a person's seat depended on his or her place within the family. The tipi camp was also set up in a circle, and each tipi had a special position within the camp.

An open doorflap signaled that visitors were welcome.

20

Children loved to sit around the tipi fire listening to stories told by **elders**.

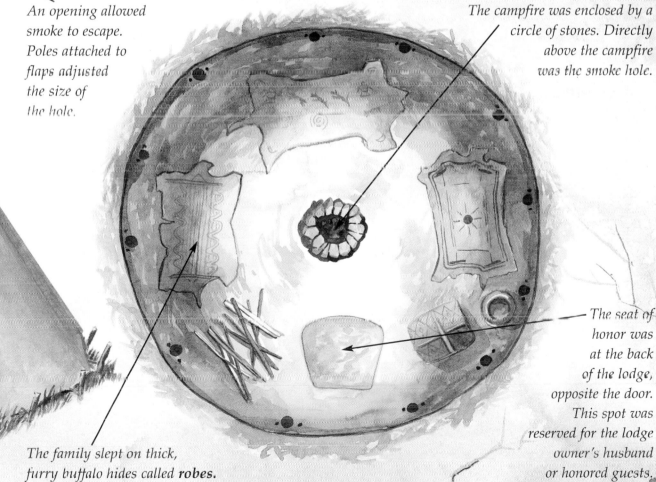

An opening allowed smoke to escape. Poles attached to flaps adjusted the size of the hole.

The campfire was enclosed by a circle of stones. Directly above the campfire was the smoke hole.

The seat of honor was at the back of the lodge, opposite the door. This spot was reserved for the lodge owner's husband or honored guests.

The family slept on thick, furry buffalo hides called **robes**.

21

Earth lodges

Some Plains nations, such as the Mandan and Hidatsa, were farmers. Although they used tipis during hunting trips, they also built permanent homes called **earth lodges**. Earth lodges were dome-shaped structures built around a wooden frame. People covered the frame with wild grass, bark, or branches and packed soil on top. Over time, grass grew on the soil, giving the lodge the appearance of a small hill.

Permanent villages

Several nations lived in earth-lodge villages. Some villages had a hundred large lodges and were surrounded by palisades or deep trenches to protect them from attacks by Plains warriors. The lodges were built in a jumbled arrangement with a central **plaza**, or open area where activities were held. Families sometimes built several lodges that were connected by covered walkways.

The main lodge was larger than the others. Women and children often slept in the attached smaller lodges, since these dwellings were easier to heat in cold weather. In winter, some people moved to villages with smaller earth lodges. These winter villages were located in sheltered valleys, where it was easier to find firewood.

© Tom Lovell

*Winters were freezing cold! The people who lived in earth lodges needed to collect a lot of firewood to stay warm. In this picture, the firewood is being transported on a carrier called a **travois**.*

Inside the earth lodge

Most lodges had a tunnel-like entrance made of a row of short wooden posts. The entrance had a door made of hide on the inner side. The tunnel kept wind from rushing inside the lodge. A fireplace was set into the floor in the center of the lodge, directly under the smoke hole in the roof. It was used for cooking and heat. Food was kept in storage pits that were dug into the earth floor, where the cool ground helped preserve it. The pits were opened only once every few days, so less air would get in and spoil the food.

Underground log lodge

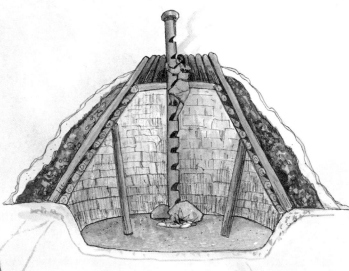

This woman uses a ladder made from a long log with notches carved on one side. The Salish man in the picture poses in front of his family lodge.

Some Cree tribes of northern Quebec and Salish nations of the American Plateau and interior British Columbia built dwellings that were similar to earth lodges. They used these lodges as their winter homes. To make the home, men dug a large circular hole and then made a framework of logs inside it that sloped in towards the top. The inside of the lodge was covered with sheets of cedar bark, and the outside was plastered with earth. In summer, these people lived in wigwams made of bark or hide.

The hogan

The **hogan** is the traditional home of the *Dineh*, or Navajo, people of the Southwest. It was made of wooden poles or logs covered with earth, clay, or thick **adobe**. Adobe is clay mixed with dried plants. It absorbs the sun's heat during the day and keeps the interior of the lodge warm at night.

Modern hogans

By 1900, railways crossed the Southwest, and the Navajo began using wooden railroad ties to build hogans. These later hogans were not covered with earth or adobe. Instead, layers of mud cemented the wooden ties together.

modern hogan

Hogans today

People still build hogans on the Navajo **reservation** and use them for ceremonial purposes. Navajo shepherds often live in hogans as well while tending their sheep on the reservation's outlying grazing land.

Hogan interiors

The hogan door traditionally faced the rising sun in the east. Inside, men sat on the south side and women on the north. Honored visitors sat in the west, facing the door. In the middle of the floor was a fireplace. Family members slept around it on fluffy sheepskins.

Pueblo "apartments"

People have been living in the Southwest for at least ten thousand years. Long ago, these people were mainly nomadic hunters who followed animal herds. People such as the Hopi and Zuni often found shelter inside caves. More than two thousand years ago, however, people learned how to farm corn. With a reliable food source, they no longer had to follow the buffalo herds.

They began building permanent homes so they could grow corn year-round. Their first permanent homes were similar to earth lodges, with a pit dug into the ground. These homes were called **pithouses**. People used this type of home for about a thousand years before they began building **pueblos**, which resembled apartment buildings. Many families lived in these large structures.

Some of the rooms in the pueblo were living rooms, and others were used as work and storage areas. As families grew, rooms were added.

26

Spanish for "towns"

Spanish priests gave these dwellings the name "pueblos," which means "towns" in Spanish. The groups who lived in them also came to be known as Pueblos. Pueblo people made beautiful pottery, which they traded with nomadic hunting nations for the meat and hides of buffalo and other animals.

Building the pueblos

Pueblo villages were sometimes built on cliffs or in caves. The houses often faced south to catch the warm afternoon sun. The roofs of the homes were held up by wooden beams.

Made of adobe

Pueblos were constructed by stacking stone slabs and adobe bricks in layers and packing mud into the grooves between them. The bricks were made of clay, grass, and ashes and were left to harden in the sun. After the bricks were in place, the walls were covered with layers of plaster and paint.

Up a ladder to the roof

To enter the pueblo, people used one ladder to get up to the roof and then climbed down into the home using another ladder. At night, the ladders were pulled up so that strangers would not be able to enter. Inside, the levels were also connected by ladders. Doors and windows were small to keep the dwellings cool during the day and warm at night.

People entered a pueblo by climbing up a ladder to the second level and then using other ladders inside.

Zuni women made pottery with intricate designs.

27

Plankhouses

For thousands of years, many nations on the Northwest Coast built large rectangular wooden homes that were richly decorated with beautiful carvings. These homes were known as **plankhouses** and, sometimes, longhouses. They were built of red cedar, which is plentiful throughout the Northwest. Cedar is an ideal building material because it splits naturally and easily in straight lines to make planks, and it does not rot in the damp climate of the Pacific Coast.

Inside the plankhouse

In the past, extended families lived together in a single plankhouse. Some houses had large central fire pits, and others had individual fireplaces for cooking meals. People hung food and animal hides from rafters and racks above the fires, so the smoke would dry and preserve them. People also stored food inside large wooden boxes. They often sat on mats of woven cedar bark.

Totem poles

Totem poles are the most distinctive feature of the homes of Northwest Coast nations. Totem poles are tall cedar trunks carved and painted to resemble a series of **totems** stacked one upon the other.

Totems are the spirits of animals and other beings, which are considered to be the ancestors or special protectors of individuals and families. Totem poles represented a family's history or accomplishments. They decorated both the interiors and exteriors of plankhouses.

Plankhouses were built in permanent villages along the coast, where fishing for food was the main occupation. Large villages were home to several hundred people. Some Northwest Coast nations had winter villages inland, near lakes or rivers in the mountains. People also made short trips inland to hunt deer and to trade the oil from the fish they caught.

Arctic homes

The Inuit have lived in the harsh Arctic region for thousands of years, where they survived by hunting. During the long winter, they hunted sea mammals such as seals and whales along the coasts. In summer, they moved inland and hunted caribou. Temporary homes suited the nomadic lifestyle of these people. During the brief summer, most lived in tents made of animal hides and whalebone poles. In winter, they built warmer, sturdier homes, such as underground **dugouts** or snow houses called **iglus** (igloos).

Iglus

Iglus are dome-shaped houses built using blocks of snow. Iglu is an Inuit word for "house," although the Inuit call iglus "igluvigak" or "ice houses." Most iglus had a single main room, but some also had smaller attached domes, which were used for storage.

A single family usually lived in each iglu, but some extended families shared a home. Sometimes families built their iglus close together and connected them with covered tunnels so they could visit one another without having to go outside.

Inside the iglu

Most iglus had three snow platforms. The family slept on the largest one. People piled moss and fur on top of the sleeping platform. One of the smaller platforms provided a workspace, and the other held the fireplace.

The fireplace was a large dish carved from soapstone and filled with animal oil. A wick of hair or moss was used to burn the oil. Wet clothing was hung from branches criss-crossed above the fire. Food was not cooked but was eaten raw.

Building an iglu

1. The builder cuts packed snow into blocks and arranges them in a circle around the hole. He tilts the blocks and cuts the tops at an angle.

2. Standing inside the circle, the builder stacks rows of blocks so they slant inward. He cuts them so they will spiral upward.

3. The last block is placed at the top, in the center of the dome. The builder then cuts a low hole in the wall so he can get out.

4. From the outside, he packs the cracks with snow and digs an entrance tunnel. People have to crawl through the tunnel to get inside the iglu.

While one man builds the iglu, another fishes through a hole in the ice so that there will be food to eat when the home is ready.

31

GLOSSARY

adobe Sun-dried clay; a home built using bricks made of sun-dried clay

band A group of Native people who live together in a village or camp

clan A large family group related by a common ancestor

elder An older, respected member of a clan

emblem An animal symbol that is important to a Native clan

hide The skin of an animal

homeland A person's native land

indigenous Describing people who are the first to live in a particular area

medicine man A healer or spiritual leader of a Native clan

nation A group of people who share origins, customs, and often, language

nomadic Describing people who move from place to place

palisade A fence made of pointed stakes

plain A large region covered with grass

Plains Relating to the Great Plains, a vast grassland region of Central North America

plaza An open, central meeting place found in some Native villages

reservation A tract of land set aside for use by Native Americans; called a reserve in Canada

sedentary Describing people who live in one place

thatch A covering made of layers of plants such as leaves, grasses, or straw

travois A French name for a device made of two poles that are attached to a horse or dog and used to transport belongings

INDEX